Cryptocurrency—

Bitcoin, Ethereum, & other

Blockchain Technology

|

How a Knowledgeable Few Will

Cash Out on This Slept On Business Opportunity

Styls Renner

Table of Contents

Disclaimer

Although the author has every intention of influencing you in a positive way, they, as well as the producer and any and all peoples involved, take no responsibility for any outcome to arise after reading this work. This publication is strictly for educational purposes. Any and all events in life requiring decisions of great magnitude should be handled with care and under guidance of a professional. The ideas and views expressed hereafter are not affiliated with any group, person or persons beyond the writer and helpful contributors. Thank you for your patience and without further ado.

Introduction

When I first started with crypto, I made many mistakes. Since then, I've realized what's important. It is paramount that as a new player you take every precaution to remember your passwords and seed. Between various exchanges, websites, and software, you'll need to understand the importance of securing your wallet. You wouldn't give up the code to your safe, and the knowledge I want to share with you can be just as valuable. When we begin you will see—no matter what your background or skill level is, I will help you. I provide a step-by-step guide for beginner investors, and I'll explain everything from common cryptocurrencies to advanced theories of blockchain.

I am writing this book because I am passionate about the emergence of cryptocurrency. From my experience and knowledge, I wish to share with you that it's not just theory. There is a world of cryptocurrency set to soon take over this world's currency. Better for you to prepare for it now.

Awareness

This guide aims to save time for those who want to know what all the fuss is about with cryptocurrencies, Bitcoin, and other digital coins. Quickly and in a simpler way via audiobook. While writing this guide, I kept in my mind a busy person who needs to know if the crypto world is a good fit for them but who doesn't have the time to go through days of researching the field. My first goal is for this guide to be your shortcut.

My second goal is to eliminate as much geeky mumbo-jumbo as possible. It's not feasible to altogether avoid the jargon when discussing a field as new as this. Every time I use a technical term in this guide, I'll first explain it in the plainest English possible. This guide won't take any previous knowledge for granted. If you're a bit techy yourself, please don't be offended if the explanations seem too obvious—I'm trying to simplify the material as much as possible to make it accessible to newcomers from all backgrounds. I firmly believe that cryptocurrency could be a great opportunity for many people who, unfortunately, are quickly put off by the usual barrier of geek speak and overly technical detail.

Honestly, cryptocurrency is not half as complex as it might seem. You can learn in a very short time if somebody weeds out the unnecessary detail and presents the basics to you in clear, actionable terms. If I become that person for you, my mission is complete. With this new understanding, you can join me on the front lines. Be that cutting edge. Crypto is the future of finance, and it's already changing the way we see the world. Whether you're interested in investing, blockchain technology, or cryptocurrency assets, there's something for everyone. With so many potential uses and so many different opportunities, the possibilities are endless.

Cryptocurrency solves many issues that have plagued the

financial sector for centuries. Generations old problems of asset management, inflation, or currency depreciation. A remarkable milestone has been reached. I'm sure you've heard it. Cryptocurrency is one of the most talked-about aspects of technology in present day conversation. Set to have a significant impact on everyone's future.

People interested in cryptocurrency, who want to learn more, will find this book helpful. I'll give you an overview of cryptocurrency and what it's capable of. We can start by learning cryptocurrency in the form of Bitcoin and something called blockchain technology. Then, we will learn about decentralized financial applications and non-fungible tokens, referred to as DeFi and NFT's respectively. By the end of our time together, you will know enough to obtain and trade various cryptocurrencies. You'll be able to confidently invest in this industry. You'll also know the fundamentals of blockchain technology and decentralized finance in order to recognize opportunity in this field when it presents itself. Whether you are an investor, a digital artist, or a novice to it all, this book will have something for every listener.

Chapter One: Cryptocurrency Origins

I'll be honest, at the start of my adventure, I was infected with skepticism. Many people terrified me by informing me that cryptocurrency was a financial pyramid, wildcat venture, or something similar. False assumptions like these keep a lot of people from achieving their goals. Just a limited number of skeptics double-check these claims, rather than taking them at face value. I was one of them.

I first heard about crypto in 2012 with the popularity of Bitcoin, a new form of digital currency which cost about $300 a coin then. I was struck with awe at the concept. It fascinated me. With no money to invest, I could only spread the word to close family and friends, hoping someone would share in the excitement and agree with my instincts. I swore that the technology behind it was the most notable advancement of the human race since sliced bread or the wheel—a bit complex but perfectly understandable when explained in the right words.

The fundamentals of cryptocurrency involve encrypting messages or information with codes so that they are hidden except for someone with accurate credentials. The word "cryptocurrency" is derived from the root words; "cryptography" and "currency." With specific authorization, you can access a portion of this information. The portion that proves Player 1 owns X-amount of

Bitcoin or Player 2 paid Y-amount of Bitcoin to Player 1. It can be more subtle as well. You can see your balance because you have the appropriate password, but no one else can without that same password.

You can have an address that someone sends Bitcoin to. Conversely, you have an address you sent Bitcoin from. This type of emerging technology is called Blockchain Technology. I'm sure you'll agree that there's something happening, and it's important enough that you will want to know as much about it now, rather than later.

Besides its basic novelty factor, cryptocurrency has another use that makes it something people want to own. When you exchange cryptocurrency, it's a person-to-person transaction. There's no bank involved. No facilitating entity that manages the transfer, a lot like a cash transaction only with your computer or phone.

Think of it as a ledger that records every transaction that happens in a never-ending log. The only way to not have a discrepancy would be if everyone had access to and shared the same records. I know what you're thinking, "Styls, how on earth could any computer have such a record? It would explode from the size of it all." That may be true, but it's not just one computer that runs this thing. It's a great multitude of computers all over the world working together to maintain the integrity of the system, like balancing the world's biggest checkbook.

There's a link to the ledger online. www.blockchainexplorer.com Obviously, I can't give it to you here, but there is one. Trust me. You could look it up, but little good it would do you if you don't understand what you're looking for. Just know that it's there. Yo4u can take comfort in the transparency of it all.

Bitcoin

Bitcoin was created by an anonymous person or group of persons known as Satoshi Nakamoto. The real identity of the computer programmer Satoshi Nakamoto is still unknown. Based on previous work, in the field of cryptography and electronic cash, Satoshi Nakamoto published a paper in 2009 titled, "Bitcoin: A Peer-to-Peer Electronic Cash System."

As a fully electronic, worldwide currency and payment system based on mathematics and cryptography, people from all over contribute their computing power to process transactions on the network. Transactions can only occur when an agreement is met by a majority, known as a confirmation. Making it almost impossible to manipulate transactions or artificially generate approval, this group oversight keeps the network safe and secure while controlling transactions.

Bitcoin can be exchanged for goods and services electronically like traditional fiat currencies. A "fiat" currency is any government provided currency given to the people without the backing of a commodity, such as gold. It's legal tender because its authenticity is declared true by the government. A good example of this would be the U.S. Dollar. Bitcoin is known as the first successful global cryptocurrency. A Bitcoin, or BTC, is valued today at over $60k. It can also be referred to and traded in a more manageable size, like mBTC, a .001 or a "one one-thousandth of" reference to a bitcoin. Its value is created by its restricted supply and demand. This is because it carries with it many incentives for its use—the most common being a market for it as well as a market of goods to be had with it. The second would be that it isn't controlled by a central government. It is decentralized, meaning no central bank, government, company, or institution controls it. A decentralized financial network is called "Defi" for short.

Bitcoin is created and transferred directly from one person to another without the need for financial intermediaries. This happens with the help of a network made of thousands of computers around the world. Bitcoin can be sent over the internet to other people, like an email. We don't think of sending international emails any differently than sending an email to someone in the same office. It's similarly true of Bitcoin.

The code is open-source. Anyone can view the code and help make improvements. When a change is suggested, the proposal is given to the network. Users of computers connected to the network vote whether to approve or reject the proposal. If there's a majority support for the proposal, the change is implemented into the system.

I know some of you must still be lost. Let me see if I can explain this a little better. Bitcoin is used like any other currency. Trade dollars or euros to obtain a fraction of a Bitcoin. Trade around

$64,000 dollars to own one whole Bitcoin all to yourself. The dollar only divides down to one penny in its simplest form. Bitcoin can be divided many more times, so as the value goes up, our dollars and euros buy less and less of one Bitcoin.

Owning Bitcoin is like having money in the bank. You can login to your bank and see you have money there. You don't have to see it truly because you know and trust it's there. The same is true with Bitcoin. You can go on your computer or phone and see you have Bitcoin, but you don't actually hold anything in your hands. With the technology for Bitcoin, you can actually have access from any device, not just your own. This is through the shared ledger of Blockchain technology. If you own Bitcoin, you will forever own Bitcoin as long as you never forget the appropriate credentials. Let's move on.

Ethereum

After the success of Bitcoin, several other cryptocurrencies followed with their own blockchain networks. The biggest success behind Bitcoin is known as Ethereum. Ethereum is an open-source software platform that works on the same technology as Bitcoin. It's the second-largest cryptocurrency in the world by market-cap. One of its co-creators, Vitalik Buterin, was just nineteen when he engineered Ethereum in 2013. Ethereum is not simply a cryptocurrency; it's also a decentralized public ledger. With the capability for all users to create, develop, and monetize applications using its native token, Ether is a payment method.

Ethereum has created one of the world's largest digital economies. With the original network running on a Proof of Work (PoW) style system, this type of mining requires massive amounts of energy. In order to become more efficient and reduce gas fees, Ethereum is planning on moving toward a Proof of Stake (PoS) style system sometime in 2022.

This may seem confusing, but what it means is: the PoS system requires miners to dedicate their hardware resources to secure the network. This is done by using large, expensive computers and high levels of electricity to verify and secure transactions on the blockchain. By moving to a PoS system, Ethereum will now verify transactions through Ethereum holders staking their coins on an exchange that is connected to the blockchain. When owners are willing to stake their coins, they are rewarded through some form of interest, similar to what a bank will pay you for allowing them to hold your money. In some cases, this interest rate can be insanely high and is usually rewarded in the form of the token staked.

When I say Ethereum has created one of the world's largest digital economies, I am referring to the other decentralized exchanges built on top of the Ethereum network. Ethereum allows other developers to build on their blockchain, creating access to exchange and swap sites where token holders can trade cryptocurrencies. Video game developers, NFT creators, as well as other creative marketplaces, can also be built upon the network. When anything is exchanged, swapped, or moved along the blockchain it burns Eth, Ethereum's native token. This is commonly referred to as a gas fee. During peak times of congestion, these gas fees can increase immensely. With the conversion to the Proof of Stake system, the hope is for these gas fees to be reduced.

Altcoins

Bitcoin and Ethereum are not the only cryptocurrencies on the block. There are more. In fact there are thousands more. Every one of them can simply be labeled "Altcoins," as in alternate coins or coins other than the two kings of the jungle, Bitcoin and Ethereum.

Even though Bitcoin has been beneficial, there are visible problems in its design that other developers feel can be improved. The high cost, volatile value, and slow speed are some of the disadvantages with Bitcoin when compared to other coins. Another may be a lack of regulation, so there are Altcoins. They've been designed to compensate for these issues. Litecoin, for instance, was designed closely to Bitcoin, except it has a much smaller footprint and a faster transaction time, while something like Monero carries more anonymity behind it. When considering purchasing Altcoins, the three main things to consider are: the team behind the project, if they are reputable, and if they are capable of delivering what they say they can. Also consider the utility of the token: is it a meme coin with no use and a lot of hype, or does it have an actual service you can see value in?

Next is the market cap size. To find the market cap size, you can take the price the coin is trading for and multiply it by the circulating supply. CoinGecko is a great place to find this information for the majority of coins. The market cap is important because if the market cap is minimal, big investors can easily manipulate the price. The benefit to a small market cap is how quickly it could grow and see massive gains in price. For Bitcoin to double in price, it would need another 1.2 trillion dollars pumped into it. For a small-cap coin worth 100 million in market cap to double, it would only take another 100 million dollars. Some of these small caps can hit a billion dollars and give you a 10X return on your money. Be careful never to follow the meme craze with money you can't afford to lose, but not all small caps are meme coins. If you can find the right ones and verify their team and utility, you can see great rewards.

We could dedicate a series of books to cover this one topic alone, but for now, just be aware there's a world of cryptocurrencies out there.

Chapter Two: Procurement

With the value of Bitcoin as high as several thousands of dollars per coin, its popularity has grown equally fast. There are two basic ways to obtain Bitcoin out in the world. You can either buy it or mine it. That's right mine, as in the coal mine or iron mine. Not quite in the same sense but close. We'll have more on mining in a little bit, but for most people purchasing cryptocurrency, online is the norm.

Exchanges

Purchasing crypto online is normally done through an online broker known as an exchange. A cryptocurrency exchange is a platform that allows users to trade in cryptocurrency: one crypto for another, fiat for crypto, or crypto for fiat. You get the idea. There are many cryptocurrency exchange platforms available, and users can choose based on their individual preference. Each exchange attempts to leverage more users through the different attractions it has. A thorough pros and cons list on exchanges is probably not hard to find on the web. A common deal breaker is what type of fee scale an exchange utilizes. Another may be what purchasing options they offer or which cryptos they deal in. Of the different exchanges, two main types stand out: centralized vs decentralized.

Centralized is the most common type. These exchanges are privately owned. Trading can only be done after the user has provided registration and identification, a process known as "Know Your Customer" or KYC for short. A form of government ID, passport, work visa, state ID, or the like is required as well as a current method of verifying the user's address when compared against the other given form of ID. One example is a utility bill. These exchanges have high trade volume and lots of activity. You can find almost any crypto here. The values of commonly traded currencies are represented by forever updating amounts found on the home and sub pages of the site. You'd find it similar to the look of the NYSE, or New York Stock Exchange, and examples include: Coinbase, Gemini, and Binance. The centralized nature of these exchanges makes them the best options for beginners.

Decentralized exchanges follow the philosophy of Bitcoin more closely. There is no centralized authority monitoring activities taking place. They wouldn't be subject to regulations of a centralized exchange. Anyone can use this platform without undergoing identity verification. They can often be a little more confusing to trade because the operations performed here are of a peer-to-peer nature. Instead of making a purchase through the management client of the site, you would be making the trade directly with another person via escrow. The site simply facilitates the escrow and becomes the establishment for finding others with whom to trade. This can be the place to purchase crypto if you are using a less common form of payment, such as Paypal, an Amazon gift card, or in person.

Aside from the exchanges, there are two other ways of procuring cryptocurrencies: through an app like CashApp or at an ATM. Not your average ATM but a Crypto ATM, also called a Bitcoin ATM. Both will require you to have a wallet to perform this. CashApp's built-in features serve as storage to house your Bitcoin. It is also, arguably, the easiest way to obtain and trade Bitcoin. Although it's terms and conditions limit deposits of Bitcoin to legal origins of transfer. No gambling site money is going here. For everything else, you need a wallet.

Wallets

A cryptocurrency wallet has a similar function to the traditional wallet in that it stores our medium of financial exchange. Traditional wallets are used to hold paper currency while crypto wallets store proof of our digital cash. Crypto wallets also store the public and private keys that are used to transact cryptocurrency. Along with the required digital signatures used to authorize transactions.

There are many types of cryptocurrency wallets, and the decision of which wallet to use depends on what a user wants and needs. Each wallet has benefits and disadvantages. Choosing which may take some research and if you're just starting out, you may try a few before you find one that works for you. There are two main types, cold and hot. As a user becomes more advanced most will eventually use a combination of the two. Always remember; no matter the level of security a wallet provides, you are the major factor that determines if your crypto remains safe.

Hot wallets are connected to the internet; they can also be called online wallets. Online wallets work on devices with internet capabilities, such as computers, smartphones, and tablets. Their convenience is for users to have access to their crypto everywhere they go. This makes it easy to carry out transactions on the fly. However, the readily available nature of the online wallet creates its vulnerability. This is because the private keys, that are responsible for the security of your wallet, are generated on the device and this device is connected to the internet. Crypto held here is less secure, and people that make use of hot wallets must ensure they enforce all security measures to avoid any problems.

Hot wallets are not designed to house large amounts of cryptocurrency. You could draw similarities between online wallets and checking accounts. Treat online wallets like checking accounts, and keep only the cryptocurrency that you want to use for active trading. The bulk of your cryptocurrency should be kept somewhere more secure.

Cold wallets are the safest option for storage. An easy description is that they're not connected to the internet. You can also call them offline wallets. This lack of internet connection reduces the risk that your crypto is exposed to. Here, the public and private key of the user is stored on a device that has no internet connection. These wallets are designed with a software that works in parallel. This makes it easy for users to see their portfolio without endangering their private key by connecting the wallet to the internet.

There are also types of cold wallets, like paper and hardware wallets. A paper wallet is the best way of ensuring the safety of cryptocurrency since it works offline and is a cold wallet that can be generated from certain websites. After your private and public keys have been generated, you will print them out on a piece of paper. You will only have access to your crypto holdings if you have that piece of paper, which is why it must be kept in a secure location.

Hardware wallets are just USB devices that can be used to secure users' private keys. There are many advantages to hardware wallets compared to hot wallets because they are unaffected by viruses that could be on computers.

Mining

Certainly mining isn't a new term to many people except for when it pertains to crypto. The conventional definition involves digging into the earth with various tools looking for mineral deposits, like water, iron, coal, and gold. This does not apply to cryptocurrencies. Here, it's much less a task performed by you and much more of one performed by your computer's hardware and software.

Your hands will not get dirty looking for treasures in the soils of the earth. With crypto, we'll just be borrowing the idea of conducting labor for reward—digital labor. Mining is the process of assisting in the computational demand of creating and adding new information to a cryptocurrency's ledger, called a blockchain.

Each crypto runs on its own blockchain, such as the Bitcoin or Ethereum blockchain. Mining is carried out on these blockchains by miners. Mining is required in order for a cryptocurrency to keep functioning. Each block in a cryptocurrency's blockchain is created by the transactions of people on the network and the miners whose computers have verified the transactions.

When cryptocurrency is exchanged from one person to another, a complex mathematical process occurs. This process is designed to not only keep the system secure but to maintain amounts and locations perfectly. Each exchange is then verified through a process of confirmations that happen across multiple machines on the network. These would be the miners. Additionally, these miners are rewarded for their efforts with fresh crypto added to the total available on the network. The whole process happens under the hood so to speak.

Verification requires a high level of computing power, and it's a competitive process. Any miner that wants to be successful must invest in adequate hardware to provide a chance for a successful mining operation. Blockchain networks have been designed to adjust the difficulty involved in mining to regulate how blocks are discovered and verified. A "block" would be a set of transactions that have just occurred and need to be verified before ultimately becoming an addition to the blockchain. The best chance at being successful in mining is to acquire specialized and powerful mining rigs. One rig will not be sufficient for any miner that wants to make profits from mining. You should know that mining hardware is often expensive; a stand alone piece of hardware could cost up to $7,000.

It's equally essential to have the technical expertise and ability needed to run a full node on a blockchain network. The inner workings of blockchain technology is not something to learn overnight, although simpler methods do exist. In order to compete, a master of this craft must have a great deal of operating skill to optimize.

The hardware that you will have to use for mining consumes a lot of electricity. This means you should be expecting to pay huge sums in electricity bills. You can reduce the amount you will have to pay for cooling mining hardware by using a cheap power source or mining in locations that have very cold climates. The conditions all miners would have to meet can sometimes be a challenge that could discourage many from mining.

Cryptocurrency mining is competitive; this occurs because the amount of blocks that you are able to solve will determine your reward. All miners are in a competition with each other to be the first to solve the math within a new block. The competition helps the cryptocurrency network because the need to discover blocks puts pressure on miners to verify quickly, which means faster transactions. This is where the mining pool comes in. Miners understand that the best chance of discovering new blocks is by having significant mining power and technical expertise. If you want to increase your mining power, you will have to acquire mining rigs. Acquiring numerous mining rigs is challenging due to the price, space, and the noise they produce. In order to increase their chances of being successful at mining, miners have decided to come together in mining pools.

All participants in a mining pool combine their processing power and channel it toward solving a block. If the effort of a mining pool is successful, they are rewarded in the form of tokens in the associated cryptocurrency. The reward would be divided among all members of the mining pool according to the processing power each has contributed or the amount of work done by each member relative to the whole pool. In some instances, all miners would have to present their Proof of Work before they can receive any reward. How the reward is shared often depends on terms that all members have agreed to and individual contributions toward mining activities. This all happens automatically once everything is set up.

If you want to be successful in cryptocurrency mining, you can decide to mine independently, or you can choose to combine your devices with other miners in a mining pool to increase your output. There are numerous mining pools, but they do not function the same way. Different mining pools are governed by different protocols. The most common type are the proportional mining pools. Here, all the members contribute to the processing power of the pool, and each one of them would obtain shares until they are successful in mining. The shares that each miner receives determines the amount of reward that each miner would receive.

The second one is the pay-per-share method. The pay-per-share method is similar to that of the proportional pool as shares are also distributed based on what each member contributes. In pay-per-share pools, miners can receive immediate payouts at any time whether a block is found or not.

Peer-to-peer mining pools are structured against centralization and utilize another blockchain to maintain the operations of the pool. This blockchain would prevent the pool from failing because of central issues. If you are mining individually, the reward obtained from mining belongs totally to you, but the probability of achieving success is very low. It is often not profitable for individuals because you have to acquire expensive hardware to be competitive. The equipment consumes a lot of electricity, and many times the bill could outweigh the potential rewards. The overhead is just too high to mine highly profitable types of crypto.

Mining pools present an opportunity for individual miners to reduce individual costs and also increase chances of success. The success rate is increased significantly by joining a mining pool. Even with your chances at mining successfully, you give up part of your autonomy in the process. You will be bound to honor the agreement you have made with other members of the pool. These terms will also determine how the rewards will be shared; sharing reward means you will make less on each block solved.

Cloud Mining

Cloud computing has revolutionized virtually every industry. It has become one of the fastest-growing technology trends since its inception, and the crypto industry is no exception. Cloud computing allows businesses or individuals to increase their server capacity, file storage, software, and processing power via the internet.

If an individual wishes to mine cryptocurrency but doesn't want to incur significant purchasing and maintenance costs, cloud mining is a viable option. Cloud mining allows individuals to purchase "hash power" from companies already running a legit mining business. Once involved in the mining pool, each participant will earn a pro-rata share of all profits based on the percentage of renting power.

There are different forms of cloud mining, one of the more popular versions is hosted mining. This allows a customer to purchase or lease mining hardware located in a miner's facility. The miner is then responsible for all maintenance, equipment upgrades, and performance of the mining rigs. In this model, customers are given direct control over their cryptocurrency. In addition, the massive community involvement ensures all costs of equipment are manageable while providing a greater chance of success.

Leased hash power is another model that is common in Altcoin mining. Computing power is leased from a mining farm, giving customers a share in the overall profits. For a customer to lease hash power, they find a cloud mining company and create an account on their website. After selecting a contract period and amount of hashing power to purchase, the customer will make their payments and secure their rewards.

Like anything, cloud mining has its advantages and disadvantages. While cloud mining can cut down on your cost significantly, it can also increase your risk. There are many scam companies out there looking to take people's information and money. When choosing to go the cloud mining route, always make sure and do your due diligence. Source the company, the individuals who own or run it, and any reviews you can find on previous customers. Linkedin is an excellent source for checking credibility. Search all the team members and make sure they are who they say they are. If involved in the right company, cloud mining may be a great way of maintaining passive income.

Chapter Three: Clearnet

The Clearnet is commonly referred to as the surface web. It is publicly available, unencrypted, and accessed through search engines. This is where you can go to Google or Yahoo and type in any sequence of keywords you want to search. Type in "cryptocurrency" and receive about 523 million results. If there is a location that you are trying to go directly, you can type a URL (Uniform Resource Location) link exactly to be delivered to the exact page of your choosing.

With this form of web browsing, all articles searched and sites accessed will remain in your history. Apps, such as Facebook and Instagram, will be able to tap into this data and use it to target ads to you through their platforms. Although there may be some gruesome, or questionable content available through this form of a search engine, it is not considered illegal or connected to the criminal underworld.

Blockchain itself can be viewed as a form of clearnet where all transactions and data movement can be openly viewed and publicly available.

Darknet

The world wide web contains a lot of information. Although this is plainly true, I'm sure you would be amazed to find out that the darknet has over 500 times the amount of information as the clearnet. None of which is easily accessed through search engines and much of it a lot darker in nature. The darknet allows users to work anonymously, keeping their identity and location restricted.

To access the dark web, a user requires custom software. A common method is through the Onion browser or the more technical term of Tor browser. Cybercriminals have started resorting to the dark web for their illegal activities and cryptocurrency to fund them. This has led to negative press for Bitcoin and other related cryptos. However, what many are unaware of is the open ledger system that Bitcoin is built on; allows authorities to be able to track such payments. In the recent case of the Colonial Pipeline hacking, authorities tracked and recovered 2.3 million dollars paid to the hackers in different forms of cryptocurrency. Some cryptocurrencies have what is referred to as a burn mechanism. Companies like Binance will burn so many tokens per quarter. This makes them deflationary and can cause the price to go up. It can also work in the event of a cybercrime, where the company can track the tokens sent through the blockchain. They can relocate the assets and burn them from the ledger, completely removing them from existence. This renders them useless and makes the cyber criminal's efforts worthless.

Although Bitcoin may not be burnable, it is 100% traceable. Every movement ever made by Bitcoin can be traced back to the exact moment it was mined. The open ledger allows public viewing to every wallet address that holds those specific tokens. When Bitcoin is used in cybercrime or criminal activity, the criminal receiving the funds will need to remove the tokens and place them in a cold storage wallet. This may seem to the thief like a way to remain anonymous and undetectable. However, the only way to turn those tokens into cash is through an exchange, or to transfer them to a person willing to pay you for them. Once the coins become active and move across the blockchain, they are easily followed. It is much easier for an illegal or illicit activity to be done through fiat money than it is a cryptocurrency. Especially any token that has the ability to be burnt by the creator.

Anonymity

A transaction in and of itself is anonymous. No information about you is logged within the publicly viewable information. What can be seen is a cryptic address of letters and numbers. If this address is somehow linked to you, then the association can constructively be produced. Say by seeing you have it written down within your personal papers. Or as transactional history on your computer. Your security is as tight or slack as you ensure.

However, if you are purchasing them using fiat currencies, like U.S dollars, then you will need to set up an account with a company that is regulated the same as other financial institutions. These regulations will require verification of identity from a driver's license, passport, or state ID. This is done before you can purchase Bitcoin with any traditional payment method. This gives Uncle Sam the inside angle on your handlings.

Let's say you purchase at an ATM, in a store, because they have those, too. You may only be required to have a phone number to purchase this way. There are cameras and attendants. If you were creative, you could go in, hoodie up, hat brim low, and burner cell to anonymous wallet, then theoretically you're clean. It's what you make it I suppose. I've found it's always best in life to not forget you are supposed to follow the rules like everyone else. Or risk being thrown out of our shared society by everyone else.

In the world of cryptocurrencies, every country has their own regulations when it comes to purchasing, as well as the tax ramifications when selling. Most, but not all crypto exchanges, ask for what is known as KYC. KYC is short for "know your customer." It makes every client verify their identity. This usually is done by sending photos of your driver's license, as well as a photo of yourself holding a document stating you are sending this photo on the exchanges behalf.

Some crypto exchanges don't ask for KYC, but they are slowly being regulated depending on the countries that allow the customer access. Binance has their own specific version for U.S. customers, and another version for the rest of the world. Some customers also use a virtual private network, also known as a VPN. This allows users to act as if they are in another country while accessing their accounts. They generally choose a VPN from a location that has lackadaisical crypto regulations, this allows users to remain anonymous. These types of actions could, however, lead to more government regulations on crypto.

Security

There is a common saying in the crypto world: "Not your keys, not your coins." What this refers to is the key phrase that comes with storage wallets. Any storage wallet you use will have keys. Whether it be a hot wallet, like Metamask or Trustwallet, or cold storage, like a Ledger Nano. They will all come with a twelve-word keyphrase that you will need to access the wallet. One of the riskier parts of cryptocurrencies is the thought of losing these keys. There are horror stories of people who have lost the keys to their wallets containing millions of dollars worth of crypto assets. When this happens, there are only a limited number of chances to get the key order correctly to regain access to your coins. Another form of security provided by exchanges is a two-factor authenticator. These are great in theory but can be easily bypassed by hackers using email and text messaging phishing scams. Once you have opened one of these invasive messages, there is a possibility the hacker has garnered access to your laptop or mobile device. So, when venturing into the crypto world, be extra cautious of what types of emails and texts you interact with.

One thing to consider when making the plunge into the crypto asset space is your long-term intentions. If you are planning on holding for any length of time, then it may be a good idea to remove your coins from the exchange you purchased them on to some form of wallet. If your intention is to be trading and scalping, then you will want to leave a good portion of them on the exchange you plan to trade on. One thing that many are unaware of is the fact that you can only add and remove so many coins a day from an exchange. Every exchange is different, but on average it is about fifty thousand dollars daily that you can move off an exchange with a standard account.

By leaving your coins on a trading account, it does leave you open to the possibility of a cybercriminal hacking the exchange. It doesn't mean that you will become a victim of the hack, but it does increase the chances. Exchanges are constantly updating and improving their security features for these purposes, but as exchanges get wiser, so do the hackers. Leaving the best and most secure option a cold storage wallet, where the coins are held entirely offline.

Chapter Four: Basics

Blockchain is the technology of a shared ledger of financial transactions that have occurred on one network. Such as the Bitcoin network. When a transaction occurs on the network, it is grouped together with other transactions into a block. This block is then linked to the previous block, which is linked to the block before it. Each successive block requires more computing power than the last as the length of the blockchain grows and grows. Computational resources donated are awarded a proportional amount of newly minted Bitcoin. This occurs through a process known as mining.

Blocks are created and linked using cryptography. This way the transaction, data, and order of blocks are encrypted and can't be altered or deleted. Blocks linked together in a chain. It's no wonder why they call it blockchain.

You may have noticed that when you transfer money between banks, the money is removed from your account but, sometimes, doesn't appear in the other bank account until days later. This is because each bank maintains a separate ledger and has to reconcile them individually.

The blockchain is a shared ledger. When Bitcoins are sent from one person to another, the transaction is reconciled on the same ledger that everyone has access to. This means that the transaction occurs instantly because the sending and receiving of the coins is processed at the same time on the same ledger. The only wait is when you initiate a transfer, you have to wait your turn to be recorded to the ledger.

Your place in line is determined by the size of your fee paid to the network. Pay more and wait less. Pay less and wait longer. Sometimes days before your transaction occurs. The coin stays in one place until transferred. It's never pending or in limbo. Feel free to cancel the transaction if it hasn't occurred yet. Once it does, it's final. It has fully passed to its recipient's hands and is ready for an immediate transfer once again. Blocks on the Bitcoin blockchain are created every ten minutes.

Everyone can view transactions all the way back to the very first. There's a lot of transparency on the Bitcoin network, which also prevents fraud. Everyone on the network can see all the transactions and check if one is valid. A blockchain works as a peer-to-peer system. A network of participants referred to as nodes adhere to strict rules, working together to communicate and validate new blocks. The new blocks created contain information from the previous block before, such as a timestamp, and all transaction data. This proves that the transaction happened at the time the new block was created, strengthening the blockchain.

Since the inception of blockchain technology, there have been many innovations and alterations that have led to the spawn of many different cryptocurrencies. The original blockchain belongs to Bitcoin and is still referred to as the unhackable and best blockchain by many.

Double spending has been an issue since the inception of digital money. Any money moved over a computer system can essentially be considered digital money. When money is moved around, it has the potential for the same token to be spent more than once, ultimately creating a form of counterfeiting. Double spending leads to costs associated with security overhead; this causes the cost of goods and services to go up. One of the biggest implications to Bitcoin and blockchain creation was to prevent this from happening.

Abilities

Blockchain is split into four main types of networks: private blockchains, public blockchains, consortium blockchains, and hybrid blockchains. Like anything else in life, each of these forms has its benefits as well as its drawbacks, with each being created for an ideal use.

A private blockchain network is restrictive. A closed network, usually under the control of a single entity. These forms of blockchain are the most efficient. By allowing only a handful of preauthorized nodes to have entry, it allows the resources of the blockchain to stay flowing freely and not become so congested. On the Ethereum blockchain, one of the issues is the low scalability and high gas fees. Ethereum allows thirteen transactions per second and uses Eth, the native token of the blockchain to move things around the Ethereum network. Imagine the Ethereum network as a major highway. With only thirteen lanes and millions of transactions trying to be processed at once, it slows the traffic down. It can, sometimes, take hours for a transaction to be processed on the network. By increasing gas fees, people can pay more money to jump to the head of the line so to speak. One of the issues is the inability to grow to scale, which increases gas fees during peak times of trading. A private network is immune to the issue of too much traffic, as it's more regulated by the creators.

As a private blockchain, you're more likely to be under more regulation, have lower fees, and less criminal activity. Unknown third parties aren't able to enter and build on the blockchain. It would be quite hard for someone to conduct money laundering or generate any form of scam coins. These blockchains are more likely to be used by companies and organizations. They're able to maintain detailed records and to keep them private.

The first form of blockchain was the public blockchain. Bitcoin was the original blockchain and helped to bring attention to distributed ledger technology. These forms of blockchain work as a Proof of Work or as a Proof of Stake. The decentralized nature is thought to give control back to the users by having each transaction verified through a consensus algorithm. Participants agree on the transactions added to the ledger, rather than a bank or centralized form of government.

Public blockchains are permissionless by nature. Anyone with an internet connection is capable of joining the network and making transactions. Access to current or past records is granted automatically and to conduct mining activities is available to anyone. Transactions on the ledger are permanent. Once a transaction occurs, it is there for the world to see. This type of information is valuable to traders as they can see when major amounts of money are flowing on and off exchanges. If a bunch of Bitcoin has moved off an exchange to a cold wallet, it means it is unable to be sold at the time and could be a major signal that the price of Bitcoin is about to go up. While the opposite rings true when a major supply of Bitcoin comes back onto an exchange. According to Christine Parizo, this is usually the signal that a bunch of Bitcoin will be sold, making the supply more liquid and causing the price to go lower.

The main advantage of a public blockchain is that they are completely free of organizations. Meaning if the creators cease to exist as Satoshi Nakamoto has done with Bitcoin, the system still functions fully and will continue to run as long as there are computers linked to it. In Parizo's article about the different blockchain technologies, she says that the major disadvantage is the scalability and slow speeds when congested. Especially when the major use for these blockchains so far is to mine and exchange cryptocurrencies. A public blockchain is also a great way for social support groups and non-governmental organizations to prove their transparency and trust. The public nature of the network allows for all of their transactions to be well apparent to donors, and etc.

Like a hybrid car will combine an electric motor with gasoline to cut down on emissions and still get the necessary power when needed, blockchains too have been merged into a more hybrid form. According to Parizo, this allows organizations to have a private permission-based system as well as the public permissionless system. Giving the creator the control of who is allowed to see what data is accessible on the blockchain.

Generally, in a hybrid system, the transaction records are not made public but can be verified if and when such a situation presents itself. All confidential information is kept inside the network but is still verifiable through a system known as a smart contract. Parizo says that even with a private entity owning the hybrid system, it is not able to alter any of the transactions.

The fourth and final form of blockchain is consortium or a federated blockchain. This works similar to the hybrid model with the private and public features, but the members are most likely organizations collaborating on a decentralized network, according to Parizo.

These types of blockchains work well for banking and payment systems as well as being ideal for the supply chain. Food or medical-related items can easily be shipped and tracked with all parties having secure access to the systems and product whereabouts.

As the increase of blockchain popularity grows, it is garnering more and more enterprise and big business support. The more it is adopted, the more likely you will be seeing it, and/or using it in your daily life without even knowing it.

Possibilities

When most people hear the term blockchain, they instantly think of cryptocurrencies. However, there is so much more to understand when it comes to the applications provided by this technology. They not only have the ability to create more transparency, but they are revolutionizing how the world does business.

The initial use of blockchain was to transfer and exchange cryptocurrencies while keeping the transactions open to the public. The open ledger changed the way people started to view money. Since its initial conception, blockchain has now become a driving force in many other aspects of a business. It allows pharmacies and doctors to share and secure medical data. Makes cross-border payments much easier and cost-effective. Allows creators to sell their artworks in the form of NFTs. Musicians and record labels can easily track their royalties. More practical supply chain and logistics monitoring, as well as anti-money laundering tracking systems. It allows easy real estate processing platforms, while also keeping our personal identity secure. By being capable of these things, blockchain also allows us a safe and unchangeable voting mechanism. Blockchain is slowly becoming the most disruptive creation since the invention of the internet.

With the real-time ledger systems, blockchain is capable of cutting down third-party fees, reducing banking costs. According to a recent article from ComputerWorld, this is about to save the world's largest banks between 8-12 billion dollars on average. If you have ever tried to transfer money from one country to another, the incurring cost can be so exorbitant that it makes the transaction not worth the money spent. Blockchain and cryptocurrency tear down borders and allow money to be sent almost instantly, for very low fees, any time day or night. If traveling in another country and becoming sick, blockchain can allow secure access to medical records immediately. When most people think of investing in cryptocurrencies, one of the biggest concerns is high volatility. One of the things that can lessen this risk, according to Conway, former associate editor at Investopedia, is to invest in the companies providing the blockchain technology to massive organizations, as opposed to just investing in the cryptocurrencies themselves.

Advancement

In the grand scheme of things, blockchain is still relatively new. Some compare where blockchain is today to where the internet was back in 1997. If that is the case, then the massive amount of growth this and the crypto industry are about to receive could be mind-blowing and financially life-altering. At its highest evaluation, the crypto market cap was 2.5 trillion dollars. Apple's market cap hovers around 2.2 trillion dollars. Of all the thousands of crypto coins available, they only combine to equal the value of one fortune 500 company.

The growth and the gains that are going to flow into this industry could be unlike anything we have seen in the history of mankind. Not only with the value that the tokens can provide, for utility and store of value, but also for what blockchain can provide for transparency, as well as security. It is the combination of these things that make blockchain and crypto one of the most slept-on investment opportunities available.

As far as being seen as an investment opportunity, less than 1% of the world's money is invested in the crypto space. Funds invested in derivatives alone total a minimum of $544 trillion and the high end is an estimate of 1.2 quadrillion dollars. If the crypto market can garner even 1% of that, it will double in size to over 5 trillion dollars. Once the majority of the world understands the crypto market and that it works both as a currency and as a form of stock exchange the amount of money that inflows will be astronomical. When I say it works as a stock exchange, I am referring to the fact that these coins are not only currencies, but they are also reputable companies providing major utility. Cryptocurrencies and blockchain will be able to take the technological industry into the future providing the elements that are currently lacking. One such evolution is the development of web 3.0.

Web 3.0

The world enjoyed an improvement in technology by the introduction of Web 2.0, which enables us to move from static desktop web pages to dynamic applications and websites. This improvement led to the introduction of Facebook, Instagram, and Uber. Mitra, blockchain speaker and educator, says that the growth of Web 2.0 occurred largely because of its important layers of innovation on mobile, social, and cloud. You can access content on the Web 2.0 if you know the location and enter the right uniform resource locator (URL).

Although internet use has come a long way before the introduction of the Web 2.0, there can still be improvements. Web 3.0 is the latest development made to the world wide web, and what makes Web 3.0 unique is its ability to be open, trustless, and permissionless. Created on open software, by an accessible community of developers, every transaction is readily available and open for public viewing. There is no trusted third party governing or watching over the transactions. Instead, participants validate transactions as a community. They do so without any permission or authorization from any outside platform.

The creation of Web 3.0 allows for people to own their own data trails, it allows us to become more efficient and eliminate the use of intermediaries. Becoming more cost-effective and putting more value back into the users and suppliers involved. Corporations, machines, and most importantly, we as individuals will cryptographically be connected with efficient machine learning algorithms. Allowing the rise of new business models and stronger fundamental markets.

Web 3.0, which was coined as the semantic web by its inventor, Tim-Berners-Lee, is built on decentralized data networks, artificial intelligence and edge computing. Databases that work on the Web 3.0 are decentralized, and they are called interPlanetary File System (IPFS). According to Mitra, these databases bring a new dimension to the world wide web. For instance, all contents on IPFS are immutable and would last forever.

Chapter Five: Decentralized Finance

DeFi (pronounced defy) is short for decentralized finance. This refers to the movement of open-source applications, services, and commodities built using blockchain technology. The incentivized aim is to replicate and replace our traditional financial systems to be without the need of an intermediate power. Issuing and borrowing, trading derivatives and securities, insurance, investments and a great many more things will all operate using decentralized applications, or dApps.

A network comprising a multitude of computers remains clear, reliable, and outside the confines of a single authority. Exchanges that are peer-to-peer, initiated, executed, and accepted in person, over the internet, or by way of a smart contract when certain requisites are satisfied—all without the need to reveal autonomous information, like your identity or whereabouts.

Originally, the majority of these platforms were built on the Ethereum network. The quickly evolving space of cryptocurrencies has since seen many new platforms become available. Blockchains, such as Binance, Cardano, Solana, and Harmony, are able to increase scalability and transaction methods upon their native platforms. What this means is that they have found ways to take what Ethereum has done and make it quicker and more efficient. In doing so, this has made transactions more cost-effective. As the DeFi space continues to grow, some of these platforms have the ability to disrupt the crypto space and may eventually see major gains as Ethereum has over the past few years.

What decentralized finance allows the world to do is essentially act as their own banking system. By staking, or pooling your crypto tokens on exchanges, you are acting as a lender. You are helping secure the network and making transactions happen faster, by leaving your tokens in a staking pool. Where a normal bank may only give you up to 2% return on your money, or in most cases, way less. Staking your tokens on a Defi network can earn you anywhere from a 3-98% return on your money. When you keep your money in a bank, it allows the bank access to loan your money to other members. They make massive profits while paying you a pittance on your holdings. DeFi takes that earning power away from the bank and returns it back to the holder.

If you look into cryptocurrency, you will see many tokens with the name "swap" involved. Pancakeswap, Uniswap, and Sushiswap are some of the more notable. These swap sites act as a way for traders to access coins that may not be accessible on their normal exchanges. What token you will need to move money across these platforms will depend on what blockchain the swap site is created on. Uniswap is built on the Ethereum network, so you will need to spend Eth to make any transactions. Pancakeswap is built on the Binance network, so you will spend BNB, the native token of Binace, to make money move across that system. Things like this give Altcoins their value and prestige. Knowing what utility a coin serves can help you find value in newly formed projects and get in before they moon. When on these swap sites, you can see places to stake, farm, or pool your tokens. Some of these will allow you to make your interest in the native coin of the swap site, or in many other alt projects. Some projects are riskier than others and may not be worth receiving as a reward for your money staked. When in doubt, you can always stake for a return in a stable coin. A stable coin is backed by a dollar value, usually in American currency. For every token, you receive the exact value of one American dollar. This is a safe way of staking, knowing that your returns will remain the same. If you were to stake on Pancakeswap and the return is in Cake tokens, there is a chance they could decrease in value with how volatile the market can be. A good stable coin that is well respected is USDC.

dApps

Many of us are familiar with apps, we use them every day. Facebook, Instagram, and Tik Tok have made their way into many cell phones and laptops. Allowing people to communicate and stay connected. The one thing about these types of apps is that they are owned and regulated by a single governing entity. When we sign up or log on to these styles of applications, we allow access to our personal data. When doing so, we give these companies the right, and permission, to do whatever they choose with this data. Have you ever wondered why when you open your Facebook, you are flooded with ads? These are more often than not based on recent clothing brands or products you have searched or talked openly about with family and friends. Data has become the most valuable asset in the world, more so than gold or oil. Companies, like Facebook, Google, and Twitter, track your searches and follow your likes and retweets to see what it is you are interested in. Then, they sell this data to companies who use it to place directly targeted ads on your phone or laptop. Most people will just click the agree button when they sign up for any app without realizing what all they are agreeing to.

A decentralized app or dApp is just that. An app created on top of a decentralized network. With the network being decentralized it runs on the standard peer-to-peer system, not giving anyone entity control. This type of system also allows the users to be in control of their own data and maintain autonomy.

With dApps being built on a blockchain, they increase security. As transactions are distributed, they are heavily encrypted, making it so there is no single central place that allows a hacker access.

The main thing as a consumer to be aware of when using any dApp is to recognize what blockchain it is built on. Ethereum fuelled dApps need to move across the Ethereum blockchain, as Binance dApps need to move through their own blockchain. One of the riskiest things about cryptocurrency is sending tokens through the wrong blockchain. There is a chance that those tokens may be lost forever. Most exchanges make it very clear what systems you are sending your tokens through, but it is up to you to be familiar with what blockchains your tokens may travel upon. Coingecko is an excellent source of information when trying to find out more about the tokens you are interested in.

Smart Contracts

Smart contract code: Ethereum houses smart contracts. Smart contracts are code-based programs on the Ethereum blockchain that can execute specific actions when their conditions are met. The executed actions could be anything ranging from acquiring an item once the requirements are met to releasing funds from the designated wallet when a certain condition is met.

Smart contracts can be written with high-level programming languages, like C++, Solidity, and JavaScript. Smart contracts written in a high-level language must be converted to low-level language. This conversion is because only humans can understand high-level language while low-level languages are for machines. The language differentiation occurs because all smart contracts are deployed and executed in the Ethereum Virtual Machine (EVM). The EVM is a computer environment that is constructed into every complete Ethereum node and can execute over a hundred numerous operation codes. Operation codes are just machine instructions that can be combined together in order to carry out any kind of task. The introduction of smart contracts has caused the development of decentralized autonomous organizations (DAOs) and a full decentralized finance ecosystem (Defi). Traditional financial services, like insurance, loans, and lending, in the decentralized finance ecosystem can be accessed via decentralized peer-to-peer applications.

NFTs

Non-fungible tokens are quickly becoming the latest craze for collectors. The massive increase in NFTs mixed with the extremely high price tags have people questioning "just what are these things." First, let's explain the word fungible. Anything fungible can be traded one for one with any other item of the same classification. The perfect example of this is currency. Whether it is a dollar you earned at work, or a dollar found on the street, or even one kept in a bed mattress, each one is worth one US dollar. This makes these items interchangeable. When a store clerk takes a dollar from you or me, they do not compare one dollar as better than the next. Each one is strictly worth a dollar.

Another key component to a fungible item is that they can be divided. A dollar can be in the form of one dollar bill or a combination of coins that total a hundred cents. DeNicola, the credit expert for Fortune 500 businesses, says that all bills are different. Some are crisp and new; some are old and worn, and they all have a different serial number that makes no difference in the value of a dollar. The bottom line is fungible goods are all created equal.

On the other hand, if something is non-fungible, it is unique and identifiable. They are not interchangeable, nor are they replaceable. An example given by DeNicola is if you are house-sitting your neighbour's cat. The cat runs away, and after days of searching, you decide to replace the cat hoping they won't notice. They come home, they notice, and you are no longer invited to Thanksgiving dinner. Although all cats are cute, no two cats are the same. This makes them non-fungible.

According to DeNicola, the difference between rarity, utility, and appearance give items their own unique identity. This in turn will give them their value. Non-fungible assets also aren't divisible. We don't collect half of a Mona Lisa or an eighth of an automobile and expect them to work efficiently or maintain their value.

In the past, people have collected rare baseball cards, famous paintings, and unique sculptures. Just like everything in life, collecting has now evolved into the digital age. With the invention of blockchain, it has allowed new forms of artwork to be created, time-stamped, and authenticated on an entirely new level. Instead of calling in the regular town authenticator with his magnifying glass to confirm that your Monet is an original, all the required data is held and encrypted on the blockchain the NFT was created on. This allows collectors to hold something one of a kind and completely authentic. It also allows new forms of creators. Athletes are now creating NFT's from famous moments or plays, and musicians are now using NTFs to design one-of-a-kind album artwork as well as for distributing concert tickets.

In most cases, NFTs are rare collector's items. Like anything collected, the value is what someone is willing to pay for it. In others, they are single-use items, like concert tickets. This prevents the ability to counterfeit such items and, in some cases, can also offer the holder a unique experience. In the case of influencer and self-help guru Gary V., his collection of NFTs, titled VeeFriends, allows holders an opportunity to do certain things. Some are entitled to a round of golf with Gary, or lifetime access to his conferences, depending on which NFT they hold. It is largely speculated that this form of NFT development will change the way celebrities and athletes interact with their fans.

Prior to NFT creation, anyone buying rare artwork had to be cautious of the fact it could be fake. With collecting cards and comics, you had to worry about maintaining their mint condition status. This left the owners of these items with expensive bills when calling in the proper people to verify artwork, and the comic and card collectors have to go through extensive regiments just to look at their collectibles. What good is a comic or card if you can't read it or look at it without its value going down? A priceless piece of art is better left in a museum for the world to see, rather than locked in a vault to protect it from thieves. With the creation of NFTs and digital display cases, these artifacts can now be viewed and shared without any worry of them being stolen or counterfeited.

There will always be something satisfying about having an item you can hold and appreciate, but there is also something to be said for the peace of mind that comes with knowing an item is yours and nobody can ever take it from you.

DEX

DEX, which means decentralized exchange, works on a peer-to-peer (p2p) network. The p2p network permits transactions to occur between two interested parties. They allow tokens to be arranged in a non-custodial manner. The aim of decentralized cryptocurrency exchange is to solve problems that are specific to centralized exchanges. If you want to use this exchange for trades, you will have to register on one of the peer-to-peer markets that they created on the blockchain. You can use these markets to carry out cryptocurrency trades with each other without any intermediaries. Users of this market can store and operate funds independently without involving any third-party.

A decentralized exchange does not have any central authority, and they are supervised either by the users or automatically. The security of items on a decentralized exchange is provided by distributed ledger technology, such as blockchain. There are many blockchains that decentralized exchanges use to maintain security, such as Ethereum, and Graphene, etc. There are two mechanisms used for DEX liquidity, which are order book matching and automated market.

Earlier on in this book, I talked about centralized exchanges that have centralized authority where the decisions are made by that authority; a popular example is coinbase. Decentralized exchanges only allow trades that involve cryptocurrency tokens. DEXs do not allow trades to occur if you want to exchange a fiat currency for a cryptocurrency and vice versa. Decentralized exchanges work with the use of smart contracts; these exchanges use an algorithm to establish the price of many cryptocurrencies. Decentralized exchanges also make use of liquidity pools, which are predominantly used by investors to lock funds in exchange in order to get rewards similar to interests. Liquidity pools help decentralized trades to facilitate trades.

Decentralized exchanges use the blockchain to record all its transactions, and these exchanges are often built on an open-source code, which means anyone interested in the code is allowed to see how it works. This allows other developers to create new projects that could compete with other exchanges after adapting to the existing code of a decentralized exchange. For example, the code of Uniswap has been adapted to create various other exchanges, like Pancakeswap and Sushiswap.

Decentralized finance is a good option if you are looking for profitable tokens in their infancy. There is a wide array of tokens offered on decentralized exchanges. It covers popular tokens, new and random tokens. This is because of the ease involved in minting a token on the Ethereum blockchain and also creating a liquidity pool for it.

Decentralized finance is your best option if you are interested in finding a profitable token in its infant stage. Decentralized exchanges provide a wide array of tokens; some are popular, some weird, and others are very random. The increase in the number of tokens available is because of the ease involved in minting a token on the Ethereum blockchain and to create a liquidity pool for it. However, if you are interested in a token, you should carry out proper research before buying one because some of the tokens available are unvetted.

All funds on decentralized exchange are stored on the wallet of each trader because it reduces the possibility of successful hacks. DEXs also reduce the possibility of counterparty risk. The counterparty risk is the possibility that one of the parties involved in a transaction might default even to the central authority. Popular decentralized exchanges will not require you to provide personal information before you are allowed access to transact on them.

Utility in the developing world: The popularity of decentralized exchanges is increasing especially those that work in developing economies because of their anonymity, speed transactions and peer-to-peer lending. This popularity occurs because some of them do not have solid banking infrastructure. DEX can be used by anyone that has a smartphone that is connected to the internet.

Some decentralized exchanges were built with a tricky user interface, and this would require the user to have some specialized knowledge to make the best use of it. If you want to use such an exchange, you must be ready to carry out a lot of research because the exchange might not be of help. You will have to leave the site and look for solutions, like a walk through or explainer. You must be adept to use such interfaces because lack of knowledge and caution could result in you making unfixable errors. An example of such an error is sending coins to the wrong wallet. Another issue that you might face is called impermanent loss as a result of pairing a volatile cryptocurrency with another one that is less volatile in a liquidity pool.

Smart contract security: The protocol of any decentralized finance is only as secure as the smart contract that provides power. The code used to create it can also have some bugs despite lengthy testing that can be exploited by hackers, which could result in the loss of tokens. Developers generally create smart contracts to work in different circumstances, which could be effective under normal situations. However, there are rare circumstances, hacks, and human factors that might not have been anticipated by the developer that could create a bug.

Risky coin: Decentralized exchanges provide a variety of tokens, and some of them are unvetted. Providing a large number of tokens also comes with a certain risk because it increases the possibility of having tokens that could be scams and schemes. For example, a token on a hot streak can suddenly be rug pulled. This occurs when the creator creates a new set of tokens that could overwhelm the liquidity pool, which reduces the value of the token. Before you buy any crypto that is new to you or crypto with new protocol, ensure you learn all you can about it. You can read white papers and check discord channels and developer twitter feeds for information.

There are many ways that you can connect to a decentralized exchange. One of those ways is by making use of crypto wallets. It could be a wallet on a web browser (Metamask) or mobile (Coinbase).

Even though you can interact with decentralized exchanges directly from a browser that was built into the Coinbase wallet, it is easier to gain access to the website by using the web browser of your computer. For example, if you want to Uniswap, you can enter its address, app.uniswap.org into your web browser, and you click *connect to a wallet.*

After you have gained access into the exchange, you will connect to a wallet, and you can do this from your wallet. There should be a QR code on your wallet for you to scan with your phone's camera. Once you have scanned the code, your wallet will be connected to the exchange.

Before you can start trading on any exchange, you will need an amount of Ethereum, which you can get from an exchange. You will need Ethereum because you will need to pay gas fees. Gas fees are needed for any transaction that will be carried out on the Ethereum blockchain. This is just the fees you will pay on an exchange, and it is different from the charges the exchange would require.

Chapter Six: Established Hustle

In December 2013 on the Bitcointalk forum, a member known as Gamekyuubi had a few too many, and in his drunken state declared, "I AM HODLING." This has led to the term HODL being used ever since. The term is used to describe long-term Bitcoin holders who refuse to sell and continue to make gains while the price goes up. It is also converted to the acronym "Hold on for dear life" when the price is going down sharply.

Just like the stock market, the crypto space is full of many forms of users. Some are day trading and scalping to make profits, others are buying assets they believe in, hoping they will moon in price. When first beginning to get into crypto, you will hear how it is volatile, and you will hear how it is destined to be the future. What you may not be prepared for is just how volatile it is, and how much utility some tokens can actually provide to our future everyday life. The swings in crypto can be insane! One minute, a token can be climbing high, and the next, you can see it lose 50% of its value. Only to be followed up a few days later by another 200% gain. This type of action can make new and inexperienced traders panic sell at the bottom and suffer from fear of missing out (FOMO) back at the top. That type of behaviour only leaves you broke.

Not everyone understands how to read trading charts, volume indicators, or has a clue what a Bollinger Band may be. For these types of investors, the best thing to do is buy large-cap projects with high utility, such as Bitcoin, Ethereum, or BNB, and hold them. If you hold these types of assets long-term, the odds are more in your favour of seeing strong gains financially. If you want to become more of a crypto trader, the first investment you should make is in the time to educate yourself on the tools needed to do so.

When trading, you will need an iron will, lots of patience, and the ability to make decisions in a split second on when to enter and exit a trade. You will need to learn how to set your price targets as well as how to properly set your stop losses. On most crypto exchanges, you are able to trade in a U.S dollar stable coin against the crypto asset you desire. This works in the same way as using the American dollar to purchase Bitcoin or other crypto assets. You simply put your suggested price you want to buy and sell your Bitcoin at, and when and if it hits those levels, your trade will be executed.

Another way of trading cryptocurrencies is similar to forex trading, where you are exchanging different currencies for each other. For example, we will use the Canadian dollar vs the American dollar. On any given day, the Canadian dollar could rise in value by a few cents. This would allow the holder to purchase more American money than usual. Then a week later, the same Canadian dollar could see its value go down by six cents. The holder could then trade their American money back in for more Canadian dollars than they originally had. It works like this in cryptocurrency as well. Where traders can pair Bitcoin or any Altcoin against each other.

During market cycles, it is not uncommon to see Bitcoin make a massive move up before any Altcoin. Many times, when this happens, what traders will do is exchange Bitcoin into Ethereum, or another Altcoin. This causes a massive influx in price to those other assets and inevitably skilled traders can make 1000% on their money in a very short time.

If your intention is to move into the crypto trading world, the best strategy would be to focus on no more than a handful of coins. Study them and get familiar with their price action. Nobody is ever going to catch every rocket to the top, or perfectly time the market on their exits and entry, but if you can become familiar with the way a few coins move, it will give you a better opportunity of success. Don't worry if coins you aren't familiar with make massive gains. The most valuable tool any crypto trader can have is an education and a strategy. Make sure to stick to your strategy, and be prepared to make the proper moves when the time comes.

Dividends

The original meaning of dividends is a position of a company's profits, which is distributed to the shareholders of that company. The profits that will be shared is determined by the board, and it represents investment rewards. Dividends could be shares, money, or property. The dividend model is also used in cryptocurrency, and it is called crypto dividends.

This traditional model of investing allows cryptocurrency holders to amass income as a result of an investment in a cryptocurrency. There are many ways that can be used to earn dividends from cryptocurrencies. For example, you can decide to HODL a dividend-paying cryptocurrency in a wallet. The success of this model depends on your ability to pick the right cryptocurrency.

Currently, there is only one registered cryptocurrency that pays out a dividend. Infinity Pool, or INP, is the only crypto that is registered with the SEC as a legal dividend producing asset. It is still very new, having launched in September 2021. The dividends for INP are paid out monthly, and with the initial presale launch, a holder was able to acquire 16,000,000 coins for 600 U.S. dollars. The first dividend was 17 U.S. dollars for that type of investment. This works out to a payment of 2.83%. With the way this crypto asset works, it actually compounds the earnings back into the investment fund. This should cause the dividend to increase month over month. One thing to be aware of before investing in any crypto asset is the team behind it, as well as the utility it provides. INP can easily be found in a Google search by typing in Infinity Pool crypto. This will allow you to look over the asset and the means to purchasing it, if you so choose.

Chapter Seven: Yield Farming

Yield farming is a practice where users get rewards for staking or lending out capital or using a protocol. The rewards generated by this practice are often substantial, and most of them are in the form of additional cryptocurrency. Yield farming is an application of decentralized finance, and its use has become more popular since the introduction of liquidity mining. Yield farming is risky because of the volatility of crypto assets.

The protocol of yield farming encourages the liquidity providers to stake or store their crypto assets in a liquidity pool that works with smart contracts in exchange for incentives. The incentives from yield farming could be a governance token, percentage of transaction fees, or interest from lenders. The returns that the providers will derive are expressed as annual percentage yield (APY). Although the best way to ensure yield farming is when the assets in the liquidity pool are worth thousands of dollars. Sometimes, this would require you to have more investors, but an increase of investors means that the value of issued returns will decrease.

Most yield farmers stake with popular Stable coins, like Tether, DAI, USD coin. Most of the popular decentralized finance work on the Ethereum network and provide governance tokens that can be used as incentives in liquidity mining. The tokens provided will be stored in liquidity pools in exchange for the provision of liquidity for decentralized exchanges.

Recently, the reward for liquidity providers from yield farming protocols has become governance tokens. The governance tokens can be traded on decentralized and centralized exchanges.

Masternode

Ethereum is a decentralized network, and the services on the network are maintained by a network of nodes similar to how the Bitcoin blockchain works. There are about 2.4 million computers in the Ethereum blockchain. The node is not closed as anyone can be part of the network if they have the right knowledge and equipment coupled with time for validating the network. There are three major types of nodes that work on the Ethereum network.

Full nodes are responsible for copying and validating all transactions on the Ethereum blockchain. They also carry out specific actions as directed by the smart contract; the smart contract instructions are called opcodes. Although some of their functions are similar, full nodes are different from miners.

Light nodes only maintain parts of the full record of the blockchain and have to ask for other parts of the record from full nodes. Just as the name of this node indicates, they can work on light devices like mobile phones. Light nodes do not need to work all the time.

Full archive nodes store the full history of the Ethereum blockchain, including previous states. These nodes can be useful tools for block explorers. The major difference between full nodes and full archive nodes is that full archive nodes can perform all functions of a full node and also compile an archive for previous states.

The Ethereum blockchain is maintained by miners, and they are responsible for discovering new blocks of transactions. If you want to travel, you are likely to keep your clothes and other belongings in a box. This is similar to the blocks on the Ethereum blockchain. The blocks here do not store clothes, but they store transactional information and other data carried out on the Ethereum blockchain. There are many miners on the Ethereum blockchain, and they all compete to be the next miner to add a new block to the chain. The competition is carried out on high-grade specialized computers with other computing equipment.

There is competition on the blockchain because the miner that adds a new block will be rewarded with transactional fees and block rewards. The block rewards are new ether coins. Whenever a block is added to the blockchain, new ether coins will be released and given to the successful miner. After a miner adds a block to the blockchain, it would be verified by the rest of the mining network to ensure that the balances are correct and there is no double-spend. Double-spending is a possibility with digital coins because they cannot be seen; it is impossible to spend fiat currencies twice. Double-spending is when someone is trying to spend a fake coin or coins that they do not have. Once the block is verified, the full nodes will make a record of the data received.

Although the Bitcoin system and the Ethereum blockchain are similar and work on the same kind of technology, there are some differences. One of those differences is that Ethereum full nodes also monitor the entire current transactional data. The full information includes the balance of each user, the full smart contract code, storage location, and any changes that will be made. This makes it more expensive to run an Ethereum node than a Bitcoin node because the Ethereum node needs more storage.

Chapter Eight: Volatile

One of the characteristics of cryptocurrency is the volatility, which can be beneficial or detrimental to crypto owners. For example, the price of Bitcoin between July 21st and 22nd differed by two thousand dollars. Between October 20th and 22nd, it made a downward swing of over six-thousand dollars. The high volatility can be a crypto trader's best friend or worse nightmare. This can be particularly troublesome for traders using leverage when trading. Just like the stock market has options trading, the crypto market allows traders to bet on which direction a crypto asset is going to go. By longing or shorting the market, you are capable of using high leverage tokens. These can sometimes be up to twenty times the amount you are trading. If you are involved in a high leverage trade and the market takes a sudden turn in the opposite direction, then you can have what crypto enthusiasts refer to as getting "rekt" happen to you. This is essentially when the market swings so far out of the confines of your trade, and you become liquidated and lose all of your assets, or at least the ones you had put up for leverage.

When heavy liquidation occurs, it sometimes causes a massive move in either direction of a crypto asset. When people short the market, they bet on it going down. When they long the market, they bet on it going up. If you are familiar with candlestick charts, you have heard the term wick. This is when an asset's price can run up or down, just for a brief second touching a new high or a low, or previous support or resistance. They don't have to stay there long; the price just has to touch that area and have one person pay the said asking price for it to be considered in that range. This can be thousands of dollars off of the current trading price. When a situation like this happens, all of the long or short positions along the way can become collateral damage. Leaving the owner of the trade losing massive amounts of money. For new traders, be very very cautious of these types of trades. You are most certainly better off trading straight up without any leverage. Even the most experienced traders will only trade with about 5% of their portfolio in leverage. Out of that 5%, they will only have 10% of it involved in any one trade at a time. The fluctuating prices of crypto assets has deterred some from considering cryptocurrencies a viable investment.

There are many factors that could cause cryptocurrencies to fluctuate. One of the factors is the effect of bad news. Although most cryptocurrencies are not controlled by the government, bad news from the government can affect the price of cryptocurrency. Other factors could be security breaches in the crypto community and the varying perception of the true value of cryptocurrency. Along with these types of scenarios, there can also be massive influxes of money from major institutions coming on or off of exchanges. The United States has recently allowed its first Bitcoin ETF; other countries, like Canada, have allowed them for years. With what people refer to as smart money being involved in crypto or any asset, it has the capabilities to move the market in either direction.

The entire crypto market cap at its highest evaluation has been around 2.5 trillion dollars. Major hedge funds, like BlackRock Capital, have over 10 trillion dollars they play with. That type of money has a lot of power when entering or exiting markets. When involving yourself in crypto trading, it is always a good idea to stay up to date on all news outlets regarding the market. The crypto market never sleeps and is traded twenty-four hours a day. A lot can happen in a short time.

Casino

Casinos are not new, and they have been in use for many years. Since casinos started, there have been many improvements to the way you can gamble with every new available technology. Casinos found their way to the internet about forty years ago, and there are now many online casinos available. Not all gambling is within the eyes of the law in different areas of the world. Take the United States for example. The US holds a vast amount of the world's financial power, yet most of if not all of gambling online is illegal. Some parts of the United States have opened up to gambling within their state, but most have strict laws forbidding it still. That's where crypto currency has made an impact.

When there's a will there's a way. I or you wouldn't be the first to learn how to spin a reel from a technically illegal location within the US. There's nothing a good VPN and some cryptocurrency can't solve. Many people online with the continental US have learned how to "mock" their location to be somewhere else. Canada, for example. This, partnered with an anonymous form of payment such as Bitcoin, makes it easy for a diehard gambler to get their fix from the comfort of their own home.

This skill can easily be learned from watching free YouTube videos. You could start with no prior knowledge and be spinning the reels like a native in only a short afternoon. I don't promote illegal actions by any means. Just for educational purposes of course. If one so desired. Cryptocurrency makes this possible.

Betting

Similar to the slot machine connoisseur, there's another past-time that isn't so acceptable to even the freest of nations. That would be the long-held art of bookie betting. Fancy a sporting event and anticipate a certain team's outcome in your mind's eye? If you wanted to put this to the test, you might find it hard in some places in the world. Where I come from, you can't login to any dog or horse track and place a bet whether it be virtual or real life. Both would be against the law. Never fear when crypto is here to save the rainy day. Like the friendly game of slots or blackjack, cryptocurrency provides the means for someone to make these wagers anonymous. Therefore, remaining law abiding as far as any prying eyes are concerned.

Chapter Nine: Takeaway

Blockchain is quickly becoming the forefront of a new technological revolution. As a result, companies are quickly trying to adapt and integrate it into their business models. One example of this is Mark Zuckerberg rebranding Facebook to Meta. With this rebranding, Meta will be running on a Web 3.0 style system, utilizing blockchain and smart contracts.

With the world moving toward these new systems, it is opening the door for many colleges and universities to integrate blockchain technology into their teachings. Currently, there has been an influx of schools around the world offering these types of programs. According to Taylor Locke, Coinbase says that the top five institutes to get a degree in blockchain technology are:

The National University of Singapore

Royal Melbourne Institute of Technology

The University of California Berkeley

The University of Zurich

Massachusetts Institute of Technology

Every one of these schools is prestigious and offers a reputable degree. So, the fact that some of the top schools in the world are creating programs to launch blockchain into the future is a tell-tale sign that the technology is here to stay. Of course, there have been many doubters and naysayers regarding Bitcoin and digital currency over the years, but few have realized that blockchain technology is a massive innovation. Blockchains, such as Ethereum and Cardano, need their native tokens to transfer information through their system. This is what gives these coins their value: the utility that the project provides and the ability to create smart contracts on the platforms. Technology has the ability to jump leaps and bounds in a short time. We are at the very beginning of what blockchain is going to give to the world.

In her article, Locke reminds us that there are many online platforms available for the unfamiliar looking to dive into blockchain and better understand the tech and where to start when building it. They range from beginner-style courses, such as Blockchain: Foundation, and use cases. Through intermediate specialization courses up to advanced Blockchain Fundamentals Certificates. Some of these courses can be completed in as little as sixteen hours. The more advanced ones take three-months. Some courses and instructors start with the basic beginnings and allow anyone with a decent understanding of mathematical principles to gain the knowledge to succeed.

Blockchain and cryptocurrencies are no longer just a fad. Instead, they are the systems that will carry us through the twenty-first century and into the next significant evolution of our technological and financial being. Anyone who enjoys technology, finance, and change should strongly consider education in blockchain technology.

Marketing

Daily, there are new discoveries that help to realize new ways to use blockchain technology. Blockchain is now an important tool to be used to improve businesses. Beneficial in many ways as it provides an alternative to the traditional system of finance. The different ways that blockchain can be used makes it versatile and useful.

You might be wondering how the versatility of blockchain affects the marketability of a business, you are on the right train of thought. There is a link, and blockchain can provide a major boost to businesses, especially through one the technology it has been used for-cryptocurrency technology. The use of blockchain is not limited to faster transactions; you can also use it as a marketing strategy.

The potential in cryptocurrency has seen it incorporated in many games. This is a massive upgrade from the traditional nature of the gaming industry where everything was centralized. What this means is that all characters, skins, weapons, and coding designed for a game can only be used on that platform because they are all owned by the developer. However, crypto gaming allows users to also own part of the game. Users cannot only own items on the game, they can also transfer rewards and purchases to other games. If you want your game to have this capability, you can design and develop it on a decentralized ledger, such as blockchain. You can either decide to develop the whole game on the blockchain or use it only for the in-game currency. The blockchain would allow all computers attached to it (nodes) to access the same information. This ensures control over the information is decentralized giving creators and users equal power and opportunity. An example is FUN Token, a gaming cryptocurrency that is also traded on major exchanges. You can sell your in-game items for fun tokens and sell them for money.

Like I mentioned earlier, the power users have here is not limited to this game; players can sell the items they own in game for money. What this means is that you can trade digital assets for cryptocurrency and get money for those cryptocurrencies. The idea that anyone can own part of a game and make money from them has made games with such capabilities more popular, and many games are incorporating it in order to market their game. The marketing ability of blockchain and cryptocurrency as an extension has also been incorporated in other aspects of technology, like websites. There are websites where users can get cryptocurrency for doing some things online. An example is the Sweat coin, where you are rewarded with Sweat coins, a cryptocurrency for just walking. You will earn 0.95 Sweat coins for one thousand steps, and everything you earn will be accumulated, and you can use it to buy real-life items like iPhones, televisions, and other gadgets. There are other applications, like Sweat coins such as LifeCoin, WellCoin, and Lympho, etc.

Coding

Coding is its own language, and to some, it can seem like it comes from an entirely different dimension. If one is interested in creating their own blockchain or crypto asset, a lot of education is involved. Different coins can provide many different utilities. Some carry a standard form of information based solely on previous and current transactions. Some can carry a wealth of coding and data that can allow you to track packages, such as VeChain. Others, like Theta, are capable of harnessing computer power to provide higher quality video streaming to sites, such as YouTube.

If looking to venture into the coding world, a good place to start may be Solidity. Solidity is a blockchain programming language created by Ethereum developer Vitalik Buterin. For experienced coders, it is said to be developer friendly and have precision accuracy, according to senior software engineer Chirag. Solidity's creation was influenced by the likes of JavaScript, Powershell, and C++. There are many forms of coding, and some can be interwoven to create the perfect dApp or crypto coin. For example, Ethereum was coded using Go, C++, and Rust. Three different applications to develop the financial highway that has led to our DeFi explosion.

The demand for blockchain engineers in 2020 was up over 517% from 2019. It is very likely to continue at a high rate for the next decade as this technology is more thoroughly adopted. As Chirag has found, if coding is something that comes natural to you, or you feel you have a solid foundation to build off of, it could be a very viable source of income.

For every cryptocurrency that has a valuable utility, there are just as many or even more that don't. These coins are commonly referred to as meme coins and consider the likes of Doge and Shiba Inu in this type of class. If you are looking to try to create the next meme phenomenon, it may be a lot easier to code than the next coin that transfers valuable medical records.

If you are curious how to learn blockchain programming, there are many online communities you can join. You can search programming tutorials or vlogs on YouTube as well as find free courses through Reddit or Telegram. The community in these spaces is growing at an accelerated rate and are usually welcoming to people of all skill sets and backgrounds.

Development

Cryptocurrencies are developed for many reasons. The first crypto, Bitcoin was developed to create a decentralized form of finance. Giving financial freedom back to the people as opposed to the banks. For many unfamiliar with the crypto space, this can seem confusing, and to many that are not so tech savvy, it can be particularly difficult to understand.

With the development of Bitcoin, the world has witnessed its first digital currency that is not backed by any country or government. This has challenged many people on the idea of who can create money and has brought to light how valuable the ability to trace transactions publicly really is. Hyper-inflation in North America is real and may already be here. While the American dollar is currently seeing its buying power diminish greatly on the world market, assets, such as Bitcoin and Ethereum, are reaching all-time highs in value.

Bitcoin remains under anonymity. Nobody knows who Satoshi Nakomoto is; however, the majority of other cryptocurrencies have open development teams. The amount of work that goes into creating and launching a serious crypto asset can take years and years. As the future moves forward and the blockchain space continues to take shape, there are many businesses looking to get into the crypto community. Some of these businesses work in the art and musical sector. They are using NFTs and different forms of cryptocurrencies to secure ticket purchases as well as ensure the items can no-longer be counterfeited. The world of crypto is not all about the money aspect, it is actually revolutionizing the way many companies do business. If you are a business owner that feels you may be better benefited by having a blockchain and crypto asset moving your data, there are many skilled development teams out there that can make this happen for you.

There are many ways to create a new cryptocurrency, but the first thing to consider is whether you want a coin or a token. A new coin will run on its own blockchain, while a token will function on an already established blockchain. Tokens generally don't have a use outside of a specific community or organization. One form of use for these types of tokens are loyalty reward programs.

To create a new blockchain from scratch takes an extensive amount of coding and skill. This is definitely the most difficult and time-consuming way to create a cryptocurrency. If you don't already have a strong understanding of coding and development, even after years of taking online courses and watching videos, you can still walk away with nothing. Another alternative is to fork an already existing blockchain. What this means is to take an already existing blockchain, alter the source code, and launch your new token. An example of a forked blockchain and currency is Litecoin. It has stemmed from the coding of Bitcoin. The third and easiest way to create a new token or currency is by building on an already existing platform, such as Ethereum. According to investing expert, Brian Nibley, Ethereum has become a hotbed for the evolution of new crypto formations. Once again, if you are not familiar with coding, there are many creation services that can do all the technicals and deliver you a fully finished project.

When looking to develop new cryptocurrencies there are seven steps to consider. If paying a third party to develop your currency, some of these steps may not be as relevant. However, it is good to be familiar with all the steps of the process.

The first step is deciding on a consensus mechanism. The two most popular forms of consensus are Proof of Stake and Proof of Work. There are many other forms, but the majority of large cap coins run off of these two systems. What a consensus mechanism does is create the process of which a network will accept or decline a certain type of transaction. The nodes in the blockchain need a code installed that will allow them to confirm the transaction is legit.

The second step is choosing a blockchain. As mentioned earlier, there are a few ways to do this via new creation, a fork, or on top of an already existing chain. Either way, the new coin or token will need a home. This can usually be decided based on your project goals.

Step three is to create your nodes. Nodes are the bloodline of all blockchain. When creating, you need to know how your nodes are going to function. Things, such as how will the hosting work, are they permissionless or permissioned? This step is one of the most crucial in how your system will function.

Step four is building the blockchain architecture. Once your blockchain is launched, there is no going back, and many things are unable to be changed. The development team needs to be 100% certain about all functions of the blockchain. Normally, things are run on a TestNet to see what problems may occur. This ensures wallet addresses are formatted properly, as well as inter-blockchain communication is running smoothly. IBC protocol is how well your blockchain will communicate with others.

The fifth step is ensuring API integration. If you include an application programming interface or API, it will give your currency a much greater chance of adoption and survival.

Step six is to actually design the interface. When doing this, keep in mind future developer updates that may need to be included as the blockchain environment advances. Make sure all data is current and servers are up-to-date so that the interface is easy to use. Otherwise, you may find your crypto is dead on launch.

The seventh and final step is to make your cryptocurrency legal. Before launch, make sure you are familiar with all laws and regulations when dealing with securities. These are generally complex issues and include regular changes and updates to laws. Nibley states that it is probably best practice to hire a lawyer when dealing with this step.

Chapter Ten: Predictions

The speculations about cryptocurrency are unlikely to end in the next months or years. This is because cryptocurrency is a relatively new investment that does not have a lot of history that can be used to predict its future. Although there are many predictions by experts, the truth is that no one really knows how the future of cryptocurrency will be shaped. This is why crypto users are advised by analysts to invest only amounts that they're willing to lose. Traditional investment methods to build wealth over a long period of time have not lost their function by any means.

The main thing to consider when moving forward with investing in any crypto is the utility it may provide. Just like Amazon was able to disrupt the distribution and shopping space, or Apple was able to change the face of technology, there are many cryptocurrencies about to do the same. The one thing many fail to consider about cryptocurrencies is how they work like currencies, but the blockchain portion is more like a tradable stock company. Most people look to Bitcoin as the main crypto asset, and by market-cap size, it is. However, there are many other cryptocurrencies to be aware of that are going to completely disrupt the business space. VeChain will change the face of the supply chain and has already garnered partnerships with BMW and Walmart. Theta is going to be intrical in the way video is uploaded and streamed and is already working with YouTube. The best thing to do when diving into the crypto asset space is to get educated on all the things blockchain is capable of, and what companies are partnered with what tokens or coins.

Digital

There have been many predictions about the fate of digital currencies; those predictions have varied based on each individual's existing belief about the technology. Majority of those who are optimistic predict that it will have a favourable future. These feelings are not shared by the pessimists. However, what we know is that this is a digital age, and decisions made during this period should reflect this fact.

We also know that various central bank authorities have started developing regulations on the use of cryptocurrency. The introduction of regulations has occurred because they have recognized that there is no way to separate the improvements provided by digital economy and digital currencies.

This points to a future where regular currencies will have a lot in common with digital currencies due to the likelihood of digital currencies becoming mainstream. The increased acclimation of the traditional financial system with the digital economy has increased the probability that cryptocurrencies would have more in common with fiat currencies than gold and silver. Not only would they have a lot in common, the advantages that cryptocurrencies provide could even make it a better investment than others.

Tangible

We have witnessed some visible financial transformations in the past, such as the change from buying pizzas with cash to the ability to buy pizzas from anywhere you are with the use of a phone. However, that was a minor transformation compared to that which cryptocurrencies are likely to bring. The advent and possibilities of cryptocurrencies has shown us that there can be a better way of conducting financial transactions. Cryptocurrencies, like Bitcoin, Ethereum, and Doge coin, have shown that they can be used for money movement. This recent discovery has generated speculations because of the increased use of this relatively new currency.

Cryptocurrency has shown itself to be the beginning of an economic transformation, which has put the world of finance at the point of a major disruption that will affect all of us. The aim of cryptocurrencies is to change the way money is viewed, and such a fundamental transformation will affect how we live. The driving force behind this transformation is likely to be central banks as they have also started developing cryptocurrencies of their own, which are more stable. Some analysts believe cryptocurrencies will cause an end to the use of physical cash.

This opinion is shared by many analysts who feel that cryptocurrencies will only get better and will redefine money, provide a medium of exchange, and store of value. This prediction was made because cryptocurrencies have shown that it can improve access to the market for unbanked people, it is more efficient and flexible and can cater to the needs of different types of customers.

The changes caused by cryptocurrencies could have had a positive or negative effect on you, but you can still choose to continue or start enjoying the benefits of cryptocurrencies. Although the future of cryptocurrency is undecided and the way it is viewed depends on personal opinions. Enthusiasts see unlimited potential while critics only see the risk involved.

References

Bloomenthal, Andrew. "Dark Web." *Investopidia*. (2021). https://www.investopedia.com/terms/d/dark-web.asp

Conway, Luke. "Blockchain Explained." *Investopidia*. (2021). https://www.investopedia.com/terms/b/blockchain.asp

Chirag. "Top 15 Programming Languages for Blockchain App Development." *Appinventiv*. (2021). https://appinventiv.com/blog/best-blockchain-programming-languages/

DeNicola, Louis. "What to Know About Non-Fungible Tokens (NFTs) - Unique Digital Assets Built on Blockchain Technology." *Insider*. (2021). https://www.businessinsider.com/nft-meaning

Locke, Taylor. "Want to Study Crypto? These are the Top 20 Universities for Blockchain, According to Coindesk." *CNBC*. (2021). https://www.cnbc.com/2021/10/07/want-to-study-crypto-top-20-universities-for-blockchain-coindesk.html

Mitra, Rajarshi. "What is Web 3.0." *Blockgeeks*. (2020). https://blockgeeks.com/guides/web-3-0/

Nibley, Brian. "How to Create Your Own Cryptocurrency: A Beginners Guide." *Sofilearn*. (2021). https://www.sofi.com/learn/content/how-to-create-your-own-cryptocurrency/

Parizo, Christine. "What are the 4 Types of Blockchain technology?" *Tech Target.* (2021). https://searchcio.techtarget.com/feature/What-are-the-4-different-types-of-blockchain-technology

Made in United States
Troutdale, OR
11/03/2026

56847400R00049